I0775309

Scan the QR code with your phone to access a complimentary PDF quiz on everything you learn from this book

Enjoy reading this book?

Take a moment to give it a shoutout by posting a review on your phone!

WELCOME to the world of | FASCINATING FACTS

Hi there, young explorers!
Welcome to a world filled with exciting and amazing
facts. This book is like a treasure chest full of fun and
interesting information, just waiting for you to discover.

Inside these pages, you'll find all kinds of facts about
animals, our planet, space, and so much more. You'll learn
about things you never knew before, and you'll be
amazed by the wonders of the world.

Facts are like little secrets about the world. They help us
understand how things work and why they are the way
they are. Plus, knowing cool facts can make you the
smartest kid in the room!

As you read this book, you'll find lots of pictures and
interesting stories about each topic. You can start from
the beginning and read all the way to the end, or you can
jump to any page that catches your eye. It's like going on
a fact-filled adventure!

The world is a big and exciting place, full of mysteries
and wonders waiting for you to discover.

Are you ready to dive into the world of fascinating
facts? Let's begin our journey together and have a blast
learning about the incredible things all around us!

HOW TO USE THIS BOOK

Hey there, curious kids! This topic is all about how to use this book to have the most fun and learn cool stuff. It's like having a map for our fact-finding adventure!

READ FROM FRONT TO BACK

You can start reading from the beginning, just like a storybook. Flip the pages one by one and explore each topic as you go along. It's a great way to make sure you don't miss anything.

JUMP TO ANY PAGE

If you're super curious about a particular topic, feel free to jump ahead to that page. This book doesn't mind if you skip around. Each page has its own exciting facts and pictures.

PICTURES ARE YOUR FRIENDS

Keep an eye out for the pictures and illustrations. They help you understand the facts better and make reading more fun. Sometimes, you can even guess what the fact is about by looking at the pictures first.

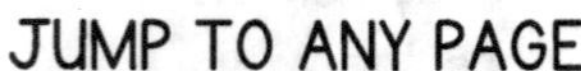

TAKE BREAKS

Don't rush through the book. Take your time to enjoy each page and really soak up the facts. You can read a little bit each day or spend a whole afternoon diving into the book. It's all up to you!

TALK ABOUT IT

After you've read a cool fact, share it with your family and friends. They might be just as amazed as you are! Talking about what you've learned is a fantastic way to remember and enjoy the facts even more.

HAVE FUN!

Most importantly, remember that learning can be super fun! So, whether you're reading alone or with someone else, let your curiosity guide you, and have a blast exploring the fascinating facts in this book.

1 | Fun Facts about You!

Your Incredible Brain

Welcome to a chapter all about you! Did you know that you are an incredible bundle of interesting facts and unique qualities? Let's explore some fascinating facts, from your amazing body to your growing interests.

Growing Taller

At your current age, you're likely getting taller every year. Your bones are growing, and your body is getting stronger. Did you know that your bones are so strong that they are even stronger than concrete? That's right!

Heart at Work

Your heart is a hardworking muscle that pumps blood throughout your body. It beats around 100,000 times every day! If you live to be 80 years old, your heart will have beaten about 3 billion times. That's a lot of love!

Taste Sensations

Your taste buds are tiny taste detectives on your tongue. You have about 10,000 of them! They can detect sweet, sour, salty, and bitter tastes. That's why you have different taste preferences.

Blinking and Breathing

You blink about 15-20 times a minute without even thinking about it. Blinking helps keep your eyes moist and clean. Breathing is also automatic. You take about 20,000 breaths every day, which provides oxygen to your body.

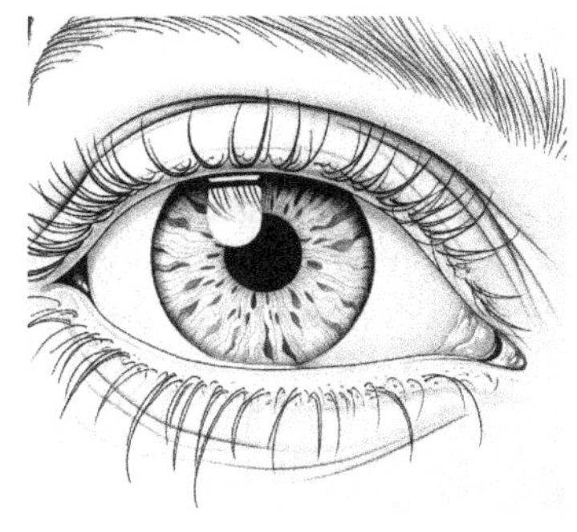

Rapid Growth

When you were a baby, you grew very quickly. In fact, you tripled your birth weight by your first birthday! Your body still grows, but not as fast. It's like nature's way of giving you time to catch up with your ever-growing interests.

Changing Interests

At your age, you might have a variety of interests, from sports to art, science to reading. Your interests can change and grow just like you! What's your favorite thing to do right now? Remember, it's okay for your interests to evolve.

Energy Galore

You have lots of energy! Your body is like a battery that never seems to run out. This energy helps you play, learn, and explore. That's why it's important to stay active and eat healthy foods to keep your energy levels up.

Learning Machine

Your brain is always learning and adapting. It's like a sponge that soaks up new information. Whether you're learning math, reading a book, or discovering new facts, your brain is always on the lookout for knowledge.

Unique You

There's no one else in the world exactly like you. You have your own personality, talents, and quirks that make you special. Embrace your uniqueness and use it to shine brightly in everything you do! So, there you have it—some fantastic facts about you! You're a remarkable child with a growing body, an inquisitive mind, and a world of possibilities ahead. Keep learning, exploring, and being the incredible person you are!

Animal Kingdom Wonders

Marvelous Mammals

Hey there, animal lovers! This topic is all about mammals, which are furry creatures that give birth to live babies. Let's discover some amazing facts:

Elephants Are Gigantic

Elephants are the largest land animals on the planet. They possess enormous size and weight, along with long trunks that they can use to grasp objects and even drink water. Interestingly, their large, floppy ears help them cool down on hot days.

Kangaroos Love to Hop

Kangaroos are special because they can hop around instead of walking or running like most animals. They have strong legs and a tail that helps them balance while they hop. It's like they have their own built-in pogo sticks!

Bats: Nighttime Flyers

Bats are truly remarkable mammals because they are the only mammals capable of sustained flight. They have wings similar to a human hand, but their fingers are long and connected by a thin sheet, allowing them to soar through the night sky. Bats are vital for our ecosystem as they help control insect populations by consuming vast numbers of insects every night. Some species of bats even pollinate flowers and disperse seeds, making them essential for plant reproduction.

Giraffes: The Tallest Terrestrial Creatures

Giraffes are truly unique mammals with their incredibly long necks and towering height. They are the tallest land animals on the planet, with some individuals reaching up to 18 feet in height! Their long necks help them reach leaves high up in trees, their primary source of food. Despite their size, giraffes are gentle and are known for their distinctive spotted coat patterns.

Cheetahs: The Super Speedy Cats

When it comes to speed, cheetahs are unmatched in the animal kingdom and can be likened to superheroes. They're capable of running at incredible speeds, similar to a car going as fast as it can! Cheetahs can reach speeds of up to 70 miles per hour, which is impressive, but only for short bursts. These sprinters use their super speed to catch their prey, such as gazelles and impalas. Unlike their roaring big cat counterparts, cheetahs communicate with each other through unique sounds and body language.

Beautiful Birds

Hello, bird enthusiasts! This topic is all about our feathered friends. Birds have feathers and lay eggs.

Colorful Parrots

Parrots are not only known for their vibrant feathers but also for their amazing ability to mimic sounds. They can copy all sorts of noises, just like a talking bird! Some parrots can even say words.

Playful Penguins:

While they may appear comical on land, penguins are graceful swimmers. Their flipper-like wings enable them to glide through the water with ease, and they possess the ability to dive to impressive depths in search of food. Watch these underwater acrobats in action!

Hummingbirds: Tiny, Flappy Wonders

Hummingbirds are tiny birds with wings that flap at an incredible rate, allowing them to hover like helicopters and pollinate flowers. They have unique and beautiful feathers with iridescent patterns and vibrant colors. Despite their small size, they are highly resilient and can thrive in various habitats. Hummingbirds have enchanted humans for centuries for their magic and beauty.

Owls: The Nighttime Whoo-hoos

Owls are amazing nighttime hunters. They have big, round eyes that help them see in the dark, and they can turn their heads around almost all the way, like a superhero! Owls can silently swoop down on their prey, thanks to their special feathers that muffle sound. They're the quiet ninjas of the bird world!

Flamingos: Fabulous Pink Waders

Flamingos are a sight to behold. These elegant creatures have long, slender legs and often stand on one leg when wading in the water – almost as if they are posing for a photo! Their feathers come in a variety of vibrant colors, ranging from pink to orange, which is due to the unique diet they consume. These social birds like to flock together, and when they take flight, it's an awe-inspiring sight to see a pink cloud soaring across the sky.

Birds are much more than just feathered creatures – they are fascinating wonders of nature! With their unique abilities and characteristics, from bright and colorful parrots to swift hummingbirds, there is always something new and exciting to discover about these creatures.

Amazing Aquatic Animals

Hi, underwater explorers! This topic is all about animals that live in the water. Some swim in the sea, and others prefer rivers and lakes. Let's dive in!

Sharks: The Ocean Kings

Sharks are the rulers of the underwater world due to their sharp teeth and powerful bodies, making them top-notch hunters. These ocean predators come in all shapes and sizes. Some can grow as large as buses, while others are as small as a school backpack!

Dolphins, the Jumping Acrobats

Dolphins, the sociable and playful creatures of the sea, are known for their acrobatic displays as they jump and flip in and out of the water. These highly intelligent mammals communicate with one another by making clicks and whistles, almost like they have their own private language.

Sea Turtles, the Ancient Swimmers

With their sturdy shells, sea turtles appear like the wise elders of the sea, moving effortlessly through the water. It's hard to believe that some sea turtles have lived longer than your own grandparents!

Jellyfish, the Graceful Floaters

Jellyfish are mesmerizing creatures that resemble beautiful, underwater blobs. Their long, flowing arms gracefully propel them through the water. However, be cautious not to touch them, as they can deliver a mild sting.

Seahorses, the Tiny Hippos of the Sea:

Seahorses are small creatures with a distinctive body structure, long snouts, and small mouths that suck tiny crustaceans and plankton. They can change color to blend in with their surroundings and are one of the few species where males carry babies. Seahorses are vital to the ecosystem, but face endangerment from overfishing, pollution, and habitat destruction. Preserving them and their ocean habitats is crucial.

Remember, the underwater world is full of incredible creatures, big and small, and they're all waiting for you to learn about and be amazed by!

3 | Our Amazing Planet

Hello there, young adventurers! We're going to embark on a journey to explore our incredible planet Earth. It's the only home we have, and it's full of fascinating facts, from its landscapes to its weather and natural wonders.

A World of Wonders

Giant Sand Mountains:

Picture colossal heaps of sand stretching up towards the sky, forming what we call deserts. In these deserts, the sand accumulates into mountains that are as high as skyscrapers!

Sky-High Mountains

Certain regions on Earth have mountains that are incredibly high, almost reaching the clouds. They resemble nature's version of skyscrapers, but with even greater heights!

Endless Ocean

When gazing at the sea, one can't help but feel a sense of infinite vastness. It's as if the ocean serves as a giant swimming pool, stretching as far as the eye can see and providing a home for countless fish and other sea creatures.

Lush Green Forests

Certain places boast lush forests filled with diverse trees and wildlife. Visiting these destinations is like entering a magical, green wonderland!

Super Old Earth

The Earth is ancient, having been around for approximately 4.54 billion years, and has undergone significant changes throughout its existence. Despite this, it has remained a constant source of wonder and amazement, providing us with a home and sustaining life for billions of years. We should do our part to protect and preserve this remarkable planet for generations to come.

Earth is an enormous playground filled with endless wonders to explore and discover. It's truly incredible, isn't it?

Land and Water

Land and Its Puzzling Pieces

Earth's land is divided into enormous pieces called continents. Think of continents like huge islands. You might have heard of some, like North America, Africa, and Asia. Each continent has its own special animals, plants, and places to explore.

Water Everywhere

Our world is full of excitement, and it's not just the land that contributes. Water bodies such as oceans, seas, and rivers add to the beauty of our planet. Lakes, on the other hand, are peaceful and serene, like Earth's own little puddles.

Sky-Scraping Everest

Mount Everest is not just a mountain; it's a sky-high giant! In fact, it's the tallest mountain on Earth. If you could stack many school buses on top of each other, you might get close to how tall it is. Climbers from all over the world dream of reaching its snowy peak. It's like a challenge only the bravest adventurers can conquer!

The planet Earth is a vast puzzle with enormous land masses known as continents, as well as numerous bodies of water, including oceans, seas, rivers, and lakes. The Pacific Ocean is the largest water body, with seemingly no end in sight. And Mount Everest, the world's highest peak, stands so tall it appears to touch the sky!

Weather Wonders

Sunny Smiles

Imagine a sunny day as Earth's way of conveying joy. The radiant sun in the sky provides warmth, enabling you to indulge in outdoor activities, sport your favorite sunglasses, and feel the sun's heat on your skin. It's almost as if the Earth is beaming at us with a warm smile!

Rainy Days

When it rains, the Earth takes a refreshing shower. Raindrops fall from the clouds, nourishing the grass and flowers, creating a happy atmosphere. It's as if the Earth is washing its face and quenching the thirst of all the plants. Although you may need an umbrella or a raincoat, splashing in puddles can be an exciting and enjoyable experience!

Stormy Stories

Although tornadoes, hurricanes, and thunderstorms may seem frightening, they serve to balance the Earth's climate. These events can be quite powerful with the wind whirling and the sky booming with thunder. Nonetheless, there's no need to worry as meteorologists are scientists who specialize in studying and predicting such events to keep us safe. Think of them as nature's weather superheroes, always on the lookout for our well-being!

Seasons Changing

Earth has seasons too! In spring, flowers bloom, and trees grow new leaves. Summer is all about the sun and warm days. In the fall, leaves turn colorful and fall from the trees. Winter brings snow and cold weather. Seasons change as Earth moves around the sun, just like you move through different grades in school.

Windy Whirlwinds

Wind is not just a playful force of nature, but an essential component of the Earth's ecosystem. It distributes seeds and pollen, transports insects and birds to new habitats, and regulates the Earth's temperature and climate through ocean currents. Without it, life on Earth would be impossible.

Changing Climates

Earth's climate varies widely across the globe. Certain regions experience year-round warmth, while others have distinct seasonal changes. Think of it as Earth having a wardrobe of its own, tailored to each part of the world. The climate is an essential factor that determines which species can survive in each area. Polar bears thrive in the cold climate, while camels are built to thrive in the hot desert.

Weather is like Earth's mood, and it can be windy, snowy, and even bring us beautiful rainbows. Earth's climate can change from place to place, and we have weather helpers like meteorologists and weather satellites to understand it all. Weather is a fascinating part of our world!

Natural Beauties

Mother Nature is a talented artist, and it has made some amazing natural wonders. These are places that are so special and beautiful that they can take your breath away!

Grand Canyon Magic

Imagine a giant crack in the ground, but it's not scary at all; it's astonishingly beautiful. This place is called the Grand Canyon. You can find it in Arizona. It's full of colors that will make your eyes wide with wonder. It's a bit like a rainbow on the ground!

Underwater Wonderland

Have you ever imagined a place so deep under the sea that you can't breathe without special gear? That's exactly where you'll find the Great Barrier Reef – a mystical underwater metropolis brimming with colorful corals and an array of sea creatures. It's as if you've discovered Earth's very own treasure chest, hidden from the world.

Northern Lights Show

Have you had the opportunity to witness the awe-inspiring Northern Lights? It's a dazzling display of a colorful curtain of lights that gracefully dances in the night sky, leaving onlookers mesmerized. These stunning lights can be seen near the North Pole, as though the Earth itself is providing us with a unique and magical light show to cherish.

Mighty Waterfalls

Let's picture a place where water cascades from a great height, producing a deafening sound and a misty haze in the surroundings. These are known as waterfalls, and one of the most renowned is Canada's Niagara Falls. Imagine it as Earth's very own magnificent water fountain, with tonnes of water splashing down!

Towering Mountains

Some parts of our planet have giant mountains that reach up so high they seem to touch the sky. Mount Fuji in Japan is one of them. These mountains are like Earth's skyscrapers, and they often have snow on top, even in the summer!

Our planet boasts an incredible array of breathtaking natural wonders, from the awe-inspiring Grand Canyon to the magnificent power of waterfalls. Earth is truly a treasure trove of beautiful places waiting for us to discover and appreciate!

Caring for Earth

Similar to how you keep your room and favorite toys in great condition, we must take care of our planet to maintain its safety, beauty, and health for all living beings residing here.

Protecting Special Places

Rainforests are akin to treasure chests, containing an abundance of vibrant flora and fauna not found elsewhere – a secret hideout of sorts. It's crucial to preserve these habitats, ensuring that the rare and incredible creatures that call them home continue to flourish.

Coral reefs are vibrant and diverse underwater cities, providing a home for various fish species. However, they are fragile and need protection to maintain their beauty and life.

The Three R's: Reduce, Reuse, Recycle

Reducing means not wasting your toys or food. When you use less of something, you're helping to keep Earth clean and healthy. For example, turning off lights when you leave a room or using both sides of a piece of paper.

You can Reuse by playing with your toys again and again. You can do the same with things like bags and containers. When we reuse, we don't need to make new things all the time, and that's good for Earth!

Recycling: A Superhero Power for Trash!
Think of recycling as giving old items a new job. With special bins for bottles, cans, and paper, these objects can be transformed into something new and useful. It's almost like having a superhero power for trash!

Earth's Amazing Puzzle

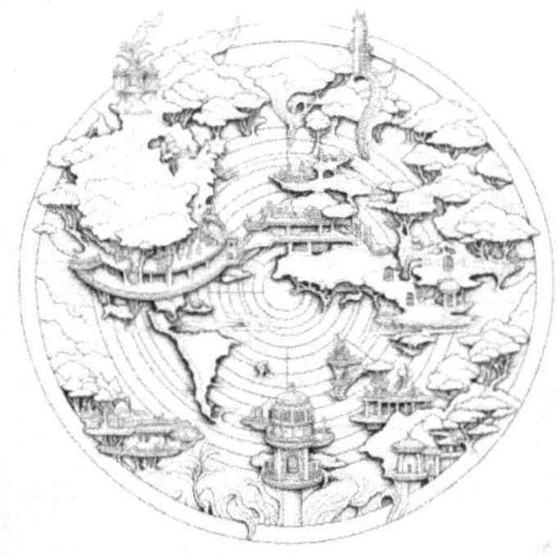

The Earth is an enormous puzzle with countless pieces, including land, water, and air, each with its own story to tell. Its wrinkles are comparable to mountains, while rivers can be seen as its veins. The secrets of our planet are waiting to be uncovered, making it an exciting and captivating experience for anyone who ventures out to explore it!

Animals such as lions, elephants, and dolphins, are part of Earth's family, too. They have special roles in our planet's puzzle. We need to protect them and their homes so they can keep playing their important parts in the puzzle.

Let's all work together to be good caretakers of our home, Earth. It's a big, wonderful puzzle, and when we take care of it, it stays safe and amazing for all of us, now and for many, many years to come!

4 | Space Oddities

Space is a place of mysteries and wonders. Let's take a journey through some of the strangest and most amazing things that exist beyond our planet. Buckle up and get ready for some space oddities!

A Universe of Stars

Imagine space as a vast, dark ocean, but instead of water, it's filled with sparkling stars. These stars are like tiny, faraway suns, and they make the night sky look like a magical, twinkling blanket.

Countless Stars

Did you know that the number of stars in space surpasses the amount of sand grains on all the beaches in the world? It's almost impossible to fathom how many stars are up there. Imagine attempting to count all the twinkling stars in the night sky, and realizing that there are far more than you could ever count.

Our Bright Sun

The Sun is the reigning superstar of our Solar System. It's incredibly bright and hot, illuminating our world with its brilliant light during the day. It resembles a massive, radiant fireball hovering in the sky. However, do not be alarmed! Despite its fiery appearance, it is situated far away from our planet, ensuring that we don't experience its heat here on Earth.

Starry Stories

The night sky is a magnificent canvas filled with twinkling stars, each with a unique story to tell. People have been connecting the stars for centuries to create pictures and narratives. It's akin to connecting the dots of a drawing, except the dots are stars scattered across the sky! Some of these stars shine brightly, while others twinkle gently, but all of them have a tale to tell.

Star Groups:

Did you know that stars occasionally congregate into constellations? These "star clubs" in the sky have been spotted by people from all over the world, who have given them unique names like the Big Dipper and Orion. These names serve as guides to locate and identify constellations in the vast night sky.

Starry Night Adventures

Looking up at the stars can be an incredible adventure. On clear nights, you can gaze at them and even create your own stories. If you want to take a closer look at stars, planets, and even the moon, some people use telescopes to get a better view.

Space is like a giant, dark ocean filled with sparkling stars. Our Sun is one of those stars, and there are so many stars in the sky that it's like trying to count grains of sand on all the world's beaches. It's a big, twinkling, starry adventure up there, just waiting for you to explore and enjoy!

As we gaze up at the night sky, it can be easy to feel small and insignificant. But the truth is that we are all connected to the stars. The elements that make up our bodies were formed in the hearts of massive stars that exploded billions of years ago. We are literally made of stardust.

Despite the vastness of space, humans have made incredible strides in exploring and understanding it. We have sent spacecraft to every planet in our solar system, and even ventured beyond our own star system. With each new discovery, we gain a deeper appreciation for the beauty and complexity of the universe.

But you don't need to be an astronaut to appreciate the wonders of space. Simply looking up at the stars on a clear night can fill you with a sense of awe and wonder. And who knows? Maybe one day, you'll be the one to make the next big discovery about our universe.

Earth and Its Neighbors

Think of Earth as your cozy home in space. But guess what? We have some neighbors, and they're not just any neighbors - they're other planets!

Eight Planet Pals

Did you know that our solar system consists of eight planets, each residing in space like Earth's friends? Similar to how you run around your favorite playground, these planets orbit around the Sun.

Mercury - The Toasty One

Picture a planet in close orbit around the sun - that's Mercury! It's comparable to a planet that's always sitting next to a warm, cozy campfire. The sun works like a colossal, scorching oven, making the planet's temperature soar to extreme heights.

Neptune - The Chilly Ice Planet

Imagine a planet that's located near the outer reaches of our solar system - Neptune! This is an ice planet that is incredibly fascinating. Due to its distance from the sun, Neptune is incredibly cold.

Planet Personalities

Each planet has its own personality. Some are big and some are small. Some are hot, and some are cold. Some have rings around them, like Saturn with its fancy hula hoop of ice and rocks!

Visiting Space Friends

Humans have sent spacecraft to visit our space friends. They've learned lots of cool things about the planets, like how Jupiter has a big red spot that's actually a giant storm, and how Venus is so hot that it can melt metal!

Earth – Our Amazing Home

Earth is like our special home in space, just the right distance from the Sun to keep us warm and cozy. It's the perfect place for us to live, with oceans, mountains, and lots of life. We should take good care of our home, just like we do with our own rooms!

Earth is our cozy home in space, with neighboring planets in our cosmic vicinity. Each planet has its own distinct personality, some hot, others cold, making space a vibrant neighborhood full of adventure.

The Mighty Moon

The Moon is Earth's special friend in space, and it's packed with cool facts!

Close to Home

The Moon is not super far away. It's like our next-door space neighbor, just about 238,855 miles from Earth. You can see it in the night sky, like a big, shiny nightlight.

Reflecting Light

Did you know that the Moon doesn't generate its own light? Rather, it reflects sunlight back to us like a massive mirror in space. This reflection is why we see it shining brightly at night.

Astronaut Adventures

Astronauts once traveled to the moon in special spaceships, leaving their footprints as evidence of their voyage. The moon, a vast and dusty playground in space, served as their destination.

Changing Looks

Did you know that the Moon is not always consistent in appearance? It transforms into various phases and shapes like a celestial chameleon. At times, it's a complete circle, while other times it's a mere sliver.

Lighter on the Moon

The Moon has its own gravity, but it's not as strong as Earth's. If you were on the Moon, you could jump really high, like a bouncy ball!

Moon Stories

For centuries, people have been captivated by the Moon and have shared countless stories about it. Some hold the belief that it's made of cheese, while others see shapes like a rabbit or a face on its surface. It's almost as if the Moon is a celestial storyteller, weaving tales that have fascinated people for generations.

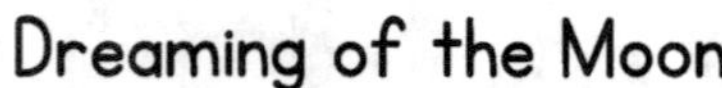

Making Ocean Waves

The Earth's oceans are greatly affected by the Moon's gravitational pull, causing the tides to rise and fall as if the Moon is greeting the ocean.

Dreaming of the Moon

When you look at the Moon, you might wonder what it's like up there. Maybe one day, you or someone you know will visit the Moon and explore its mysteries!

The Moon has always been a friendly face in the vast expanse of space, accompanying Earth and illuminating our nights. It has a rich history of adventure and folklore, and with the future ahead of us, who knows what thrilling experiences we may have on its surface.

Shooting Stars and Comets

Have you ever wondered about the origin of shooting stars? These dazzling displays are actually small space rocks that heat up and shine as they zoom through our sky, creating a spectacular show. However, despite their name, these shooting stars are not stars at all – just tiny, luminous pebbles from space.

Comets – Icy Space Snowballs

Let's take a moment to imagine something extraordinary, like a glittering snowball drifting through space. That, my friends, is a comet! These celestial bodies originate in the farthest corners of the universe and, upon approaching our sun, begin to thaw slightly. As they melt, they leave behind a luminous trail, almost like a cosmic sparkly residue.

Comet Tails and Shooting Star Streaks:

The beauty of comet tails is comparable to long, flowing dresses that comets wear. These stunning tails can extend for millions of miles. In contrast, shooting star streaks are quick, bright dashes across the sky. Regardless of their differences, both of these celestial occurrences are truly breathtaking to witness in the night sky.

Wishes on Shooting Stars

Have you ever heard that if you make a wish when you see a shooting star, it might come true? It's a fun tradition! People imagine their wishes traveling to the stars in the sky.

Space Wanderers

Comets and shooting stars are cosmic nomads, journeying through the universe and gracing the night sky with a touch of enchantment as they pass through different parts of space.

Space Rocks and Cosmic Snowballs

Don't forget, shooting stars are minuscule space rocks that radiate light as they soar through the sky. Meanwhile, comets are made up of frozen dust and gas, leaving behind a shimmering trail as they travel through the vastness of space. The night sky is brimming with these celestial marvels, ready for you to gaze in awe or make a wish upon.

Black Holes and Galaxies

Space is full of wonders, including black holes and galaxies that are truly awe-inspiring. We're here to guide you and make it easy to comprehend these fascinating phenomena.

Mysterious Black Holes

Envision a location in space where gravity is so intense that even light cannot escape. This is a black hole – a cosmic force that acts like a vacuum cleaner, drawing in anything that is too close. Black holes remain one of the most significant enigmas of space exploration!

Gigantic Galaxies

Galaxies are similar to cities, but with structures that are entirely distinct from our planet. They're enormous cosmic cities that house an array of celestial bodies, stars, and planets. For instance, the Milky Way can be seen as a city with billions of glittering lights, each representing a unique star in the galaxy.

The Milky Way Adventure

Our solar system, including the Sun and Earth, exists in the Milky Way galaxy. It's a vast cosmic neighborhood, containing an endless number of planets and stars. It's fascinating to think about the sheer amount of twinkling stars that reside within the Milky Way.

Space, the Never-Ending Adventure

Space is a never-ending journey, a vast and infinite storybook filled with countless surprises and wondrous discoveries, waiting to be uncovered at every corner of the universe. When you look up at the night sky, you're only catching a glimpse of the enormous expedition.

Dream Big and Explore

Don't stop dreaming! Who knows, you could become one of the fearless explorers who journey to space on rockets, just like in the movies. The universe is full of unexpected marvels and secrets waiting to be uncovered. Keep your eyes on the stars and see where they take you!

5 | Cool Creatures Under the Sea

Hey there, ocean adventurers! This topic is all about the amazing world beneath the waves. Get ready to dive into the deep sea and meet some incredible marine creatures!

Majestic Manta Rays

With their enormous wings, manta rays almost appear as if they are soaring through the ocean depths. These creatures are known for their gentle nature as they glide through the water, sometimes even breaching the surface in a stunning display.

Tiny Sea Slugs

With their stunning range of colors and patterns, sea slugs are the haute couture of the ocean. These creatures are so bold that some even consume toxic jellyfish and utilize their stinging cells for self-defense.

Chatty Humpback Whales

These magnificent creatures are known for their singing abilities, using intricate songs to communicate with their counterparts over long distances. These sounds can travel for miles underwater and are whales' way of greeting one another in the vastness of the ocean.

Bioluminescent Fireworks

Several sea creatures can put on a light show like no other. They generate their own light through a process known as bioluminescence. Firefly squids and particular species of jellyfish light up the ocean's depths with their dazzling glow, resembling a spectacular display of fireworks.

Playful Sea Otters

Sea otters are known for their playful nature and are often observed floating on their backs, using their bellies as makeshift tables to indulge in their favorite snacks, such as clams and crabs. These charming creatures are also fond of playtime, often amusing themselves by juggling rocks or engaging in a game of hide-and-seek with their peers.

Electric Eels

Electric eels are the living batteries of the underwater world, capable of generating powerful electric shocks to capture prey or protect themselves against predators. It's a superpower that comes in handy when navigating the ocean!

Masters of Camouflage – Cuttlefish

Cuttlefish possess an extraordinary gift – they can change both their color and texture to blend seamlessly into their surroundings. This remarkable ability enables them to evade predators and approach prey undetected, making them the ultimate masters of ocean camouflage.

Clever Crabs

Many people don't know that crabs come in a variety of shapes and sizes. These creatures play a crucial role in shaping the structure of the seabed. Some crabs are skilled at building intricate tunnels, while others possess powerful claws to capture their prey.

Clever Octopuses

Octopuses are renowned for their intelligence and adaptability. These sea creatures are like wizards, using their shape-shifting abilities to seamlessly blend into their environment. With their eight arms, they possess the ability to solve puzzles, open jars, and escape from tight spots with ease. Their camouflage skills make them the true rulers of the ocean.

Tiny Seahorses

Observe the majestic underwater dance of the tiny, delicate seahorse. These creatures use their curly tails to anchor themselves to seagrasses and corals, swaying gently with the ocean currents. Interestingly, male seahorses are unique in that they carry their offspring in a special pouch on their bellies, much like a human baby carrier!

The Mysterious Deep-Sea

The ocean's depths remain largely unexplored, containing a world filled with strange and mysterious creatures. The deep-sea is a haven for some of the most peculiar beings on our planet, including anglerfish with glowing lures and blobfish with amusing faces.

Oddly Unique Sea Cucumbers

Sea cucumbers are the ocean floor's equivalent of vacuum cleaners. They consume small food particles to maintain cleanliness. However, they have a peculiar defense mechanism - when threatened, they can shoot out adhesive threads, almost like an illusionist's trick, to distract predators!

Graceful Manatees

Manatees are known for their gentle nature, making them one of the most peaceful creatures in the underwater world. They leisurely glide through the water while munching on seagrass and other vegetation. These calm animals are often referred to as "sea cows."

Color-Changing Cuttlefish

Cuttlefish possess an extraordinary ability to adapt to their environment, making them the ultimate camouflage experts. They can alter their color and texture, appearing as though they are wearing invisibility cloaks. This incredible talent helps them to blend in with their surroundings and evade both predators and prey.

Tiny Clownfish with a Big Personality

Clownfish are known for their vibrant colors and playful personalities. They reside among the stinging tentacles of sea anemones, which serve as their protective shield against predators.

The Deep-Sea's Mystery

The ocean's depths are a mysterious world filled with extraordinary creatures that hide in the shadows. From deep-sea anglerfish with glowing lures to blobfish with amusing faces, the deep-sea is home to some of the most peculiar beings on our planet.

Curious Crustaceans – Hermit Crabs

Hermit crabs are fascinating creatures that roam the ocean floor. Unlike other sea creatures, they do not have hard shells of their own, so they have to rely on empty snail shells to protect their soft bodies. As they mature and grow in size, they venture out to find larger shells to call their new abode.

Tiny Tadpoles of the Sea – Sea Butterfly

Sea butterflies, also known as swimming snails, may be small in size, but they are graceful swimmers of the oceans. With their special wing-like appendages, they elegantly glide through the water, sometimes gathering in swarms.

Clam Gardens

Clams, those unassuming mollusks that quietly inhabit the ocean's depths, are, in their own way, the architects of the underwater world. These remarkable creatures employ their unique digging prowess to carve out a niche for themselves in the sandy ocean floor.

Clams create a small opening through which they filter food and water, forming a system of survival that also serves as the foundation for an interconnected network of underwater gardens.

Lively Lobsters

Lobsters use their strong claws to carve intricate tunnels and burrows, creating a network of hidden passageways in the ocean. These serve as sanctuaries for their kind, offering shelter and protection.

Lobsters are skilled at creating secure hideaways and are known for their delectable taste, making them popular with seafood enthusiasts worldwide for their sweet, succulent flavor and tender texture, often served in fine dining establishments and backyard seafood feasts.

The Never-Ending Wonder

The ocean is a vast and fascinating realm, full of unique creatures and mysteries waiting to be discovered. It's an endless adventure that never ceases to amaze, whether you're a marine biologist, underwater photographer, or simply have a love for the sea.

Discover the wonders of the ocean's depths, from vibrant coral reefs and playful dolphins to ingenious creatures like cuttlefish and mantis shrimp. The deep sea is a mysterious place full of enigmas like giant squids and ancient coelacanths, as well as eerie bioluminescence from anglerfish.

The ocean is a laboratory for marine biologists, a canvas for underwater photographers, and a source of inspiration and solace for sea enthusiasts. Its tides and waves invite exploration and appreciation of the planet's wonders.

6 | Prehistoric Pals

Hello, young time travelers! In this topic, we're going to step back in time and meet some incredible creatures that lived on Earth long before we did. These are your prehistoric pals, and they're more fascinating than you can imagine!

Dinosaurs, the Giants of the Past

Dinosaurs were like Earth's ancient giants, but they came in all sorts of sizes. Some were small, like chickens, while others were super tall, even taller than the tallest buildings you might see in the city! Let's talk about one of the most famous dinosaurs, the Tyrannosaurus Rex, or T-Rex for short.

The T-Rex was massive and powerful, with really sharp teeth and a big mouth. It could be as long as a school bus and as tall as a two-story house. But here's something funny: the T-Rex had really tiny arms! Imagine a big, strong dinosaur with arms that looked like a T-Rex's tiny ones – it's a bit silly! Even with those small arms, the T-Rex was a fearsome predator and one of the kings of its time.

Dinosaurs, whether big or small, played important roles in their ancient worlds. They helped keep nature in balance, just like how lions and tigers do in today's world. Some ate plants, some ate other animals, and they all had their jobs in their prehistoric neighborhoods.

Learning about these amazing creatures helps us understand our planet's history and how life has changed over a very, very long time. Dinosaurs, with their different sizes and shapes, are like pieces of a puzzle that help us learn about the incredible story of Earth!

Flying Reptiles: The Astonishing World of Pterosaurs

Throughout the history of Earth, there were creatures that defied gravity with such grace that they were not bound to the ground. Pterosaurs were one such creature that took to the skies with remarkable elegance, surpassing even the most fantastical tales of dragons. These flying reptiles were a marvel to behold, and the term 'pterosaur' encapsulates the awe-inspiring world of these extraordinary creatures. These colossal winged beings could give mythical dragons a run for their money – except, of course, that these majestic creatures were real.

The pterosaurs were a captivating species that once roamed the Earth. These creatures were truly remarkable, with some having wingspans as wide as a school bus. Their enormous wings allowed them to glide through ancient skies with a grace and power similar to that of modern-day birds. It must have been an awe-inspiring sight to witness these majestic creatures soar above prehistoric landscapes, a reminder that the skies were not just for the birds.

Pterosaurs had strong, agile wings that allowed them to travel long distances during the age of dinosaurs. Their wings enabled both powered flight and efficient gliding, allowing them to thrive in diverse environments alongside other creatures of their time.

It's worth mentioning that pterosaurs came in a wide range of sizes and shapes. From small and delicate species with wingspans similar to that of a seagull to the massive pterosaurs whose wings stretched across the sky like living bridges, their variety was remarkable. Some pterosaurs, like Pteranodon, had unique crests on their heads while others had peculiar and fascinating modifications, like long, toothy jaws.

In the prehistoric era, these winged wonders occupied a distinctive ecological role. From being skilled fishers, diving into ancient seas to catch their aquatic prey, to adeptly hunting terrestrial creatures or scavenging for food, pterosaurs were a diverse group of reptiles. Their fossils offer a glimpse into a bygone era, where pterosaurs contributed to the intricate web of ancient ecosystems teeming with life.

Exploring the world of pterosaurs, it's apparent that these flying reptiles were not just fantastical creatures, but instead, incredible products of evolution. The artifacts they left behind continue to inspire curiosity and wonder in those who seek to understand the captivating narratives preserved in the rocks and sediments of Earth's deep past. The grandeur and magnificence of these creatures serve as a reminder that the history of life on our planet is replete with a fascinating diversity that never ceases to amaze.

Swimming Giants: Marine Reptiles

Hey there, did you know that a long time ago, there were some really big and cool creatures living in the oceans? They were called marine reptiles, and two of the famous ones were the Plesiosaurus and the Mosasaurus.

The Plesiosaurus was like a sea ballet dancer. It had a super long neck and used it to catch fish underwater. With its four flippers, it could swim gracefully.

Now, the Mosasaurus was like a sea T-Rex! It had really sharp teeth and a strong tail to swim fast. It was like the king of the ancient oceans and loved to hunt for food.

These big marine reptiles remind us that the oceans have always been home to amazing creatures. They show us how cool and diverse life on Earth has been, even way back then!

Furry Mammoths and Saber-Toothed Cats

First, we've got the mammoths. These big buddies looked a lot like the elephants you might see in the zoo, but they were much hairier and had long, curved tusks, kind of like giant, twisted teeth. They roamed around and lived in places with cold weather. Imagine having a furry elephant as your friend!

The saber-toothed cats are cool cats with long, curved teeth that looked like swords or ninja claws. They used these teeth to catch their dinner, just like how modern-day cats use their sharp claws to catch mice. These cats were like the superheroes of the ancient animal world, with their special teeth helping them survive in a world full of challenges.

So, whether it's the shaggy mammoths or the ninja-like saber-toothed cats, these creatures show us how diverse and interesting the animals on our planet have been throughout history!

Ankylosaurus and the Tiny Traveler: A Prehistoric Partnership

Imagine a colossal Ankylosaurus, a dinosaur known for its impressive armor plating and club-like tail capable of delivering devastating blows. Despite their intimidating appearance, these gentle giants formed an unexpected and heartwarming bond with a small bird called the Archaeopteryx. This prehistoric friendship provides a fascinating glimpse into the complex network of symbiotic relationships that once flourished in the ancient ecosystems of our planet.

With its armored body, the Ankylosaurus was a true titan of its time, wandering prehistoric landscapes with ease. This hulking herbivore relied on its robust armor and powerful tail to fend off the threats of the Cretaceous period. Though its appearance was intimidating, the Ankylosaurus had a softer side when it came to an unlikely companion.

Meet the Archaeopteryx, one of the earliest-known birds and a remarkable feat of evolution. This feathered flyer found an ingenious way to thrive by hitching a ride on the back of the Ankylosaurus. But it wasn't just for the ride. The Archaeopteryx had a crucial role to play - grooming its massive companion. This mutually beneficial arrangement helped both creatures flourish in their respective habitats.

Millions of years ago, the Ankylosaurus and Archaeopteryx teamed up for mutual benefits. The Ankylosaurus provided a secure and mobile perch for the bird, who had an excellent view of potential threats and food sources as the dinosaur roamed. In turn, the Archaeopteryx took care of the dinosaur by removing ticks and other irritants from its sensitive skin, thus ensuring its well-being.

The relationship between Ankylosaurus and Archaeopteryx is a fascinating example of how different species can coexist and support one another in the natural world. The Ankylosaurus offered safety and mobility to the Archaeopteryx while the tiny bird groomed and cared for the dinosaur, guaranteeing its comfort and well-being.

The tale of Ankylosaurus and Archaeopteryx serves as a poignant reminder of the complex interrelationships that existed in Earth's ancient ecosystems. It highlights the significance of adaptability and cooperation, which have been vital components in the success of evolution throughout history. During a period marked by monumental creatures and dramatic environmental changes, this prehistoric alliance stands as a testament to the long-lasting influence of symbiosis in the natural world.

Crocodile Cleaning Crew: An Ancient Dental Hygiene Partnership

Although crocodiles are known for their predatory and stealthy nature in today's world, they had an unexpected alliance with a small species of fish called :"cleaner fish" in the past. This peculiar relationship sheds light on the complexities of prehistoric ecosystems and how different species worked together for their common good.

Picture a ferocious crocodile, a prehistoric behemoth that once dominated the ancient waterways. Despite their intimidating reputation, these colossal reptiles weren't against forming extraordinary relationships with their aquatic friends. Enter the cleaner fish – small yet hardworking – the key players in this remarkable partnership. Equipped with specialized adaptations, these fish would fearlessly swim into the crocodile's daunting jaws to perform a risky – but necessary – task: dental cleaning.

Astonishingly, the idea of a "mobile dental cleaning service" for crocodiles was a reality in ancient ecosystems. Fearless cleaner fish approached these massive reptiles' toothy maws without hesitation. Their dual purpose was to extract any lodged food between the crocodile's teeth and to nibble away at any parasites or troublesome organisms that may have taken up residence within the reptile's mouth.

The crocodiles didn't seem to mind the unorthodox practice and may have even enjoyed it. Instead of perceiving the cleaner fish as prey, these ancient reptiles permitted them to enter their mouths, acknowledging the benefits of having their oral hygiene taken care of by these tiny assistants. This interaction between predator and cleaner fish highlights the versatility and ingenuity of both groups, demonstrating the incredible ways that creatures from different categories can develop mutually beneficial relationships.

The relationship between crocodiles and cleaner fish is a testament to the diverse and intricate ways in which life has thrived throughout Earth's history. This unique bond reminds us that even in a world of predators and prey, nature is full of unexpected partnerships. These partnerships highlight the complexity of ancient ecosystems, where species evolved to fill specialized niches. They also demonstrate the importance of cooperation and interdependence in the natural world. In essence, the curious relationship between crocodiles and cleaner fish underscores the intricacy of life's interconnected web.

7 | Incredible Inventions

Hey there, future inventors! In this topic, we're going to explore some of the most amazing inventions ever created and learn about the brilliant people behind them. Get ready to be inspired by the incredible world of innovation!

Inventions are similar to magical ideas that emerge from the depths of human imagination, with the power to transform the way we live. These ingenious creations are born from the minds of visionaries and problem solvers called inventors, who have the unique ability to dream up and bring to life extraordinary things that shape the course of history.

Let's travel back in time to an era before cars and smartphones – when handwritten letters and horse-drawn transportation were the norm. This simpler time underwent a significant transformation thanks to the pioneering work of inventors. One such story is of the visionary Wright brothers, Orville and Wilbur, who dared to dream of humans soaring through the skies like birds.

The concept of flight was once thought to be just a legend, but the Wright brothers refused to let this notion ground them. They envisioned soaring through the skies and, through experimentation, determination, and innovation, they made this dream a reality. Using wood, fabric, and an engine, they constructed the first airplane – a true engineering marvel. This invention paved the way for air travel, making the world more connected and the dream of flight a reality. Thanks to their pioneering spirit, we can now travel across the globe in just a few hours.

The airplane is just one of many examples of how humans can use their creativity to enhance their way of life. These tangible results of human ingenuity and innovation drive us forward into the future, improving efficiency, comfort, and enjoyment. Not only do these inventions open up new possibilities, but they also allow us to achieve incredible feats and explore uncharted territories.

Have you ever considered the infinite possibilities that the world of inventions holds? You, too, have the potential to make your mark in the legacy of human innovation. The history of inventions is rich with imagination and creation, and you can be a part of it too. Who knows, maybe someday you will come up with an idea that will change the way we live, work, or play. Inventions are not a thing of the past, they continue to shape our present, and hold the promise of an amazing, transformative future.
Dare to be creative, dream big, and you may just be the next inventor to shape the world and make it a better, more captivating place for us all.

The Telephone by Alexander Graham Bell: A Revolution in Communication

Alexander Graham Bell's telephone transformed communication. Before phones, reaching faraway friends was tough–letters took time, and travel was needed.

But then, Bell made the telephone! It's a magical thing that lets us talk to people far away quickly. Just lift the phone, dial a number, and hear your friend's voice, even if they're far.

The telephone is special; it helps people connect, no matter how far. Bell's invention is a game-changer. When you use your phone, thank Bell for making it possible!

And guess what? The telephone isn't just for friends. It's everywhere! Businesses use it to make quick decisions, and teachers use it for distant learning. Families far apart can share happy and sad moments.

So, the telephone changed the world. Thanks to Bell, we live in a global village where everyone can talk, no matter where they are! The next time you pick up your phone, think about how Bell's invention connects us in ways he could only dream of!

The Magic of Electricity: Illuminating Our World with Thomas Edison's Light Bulb

Thomas Edison was a really smart inventor. He created something amazing called the light bulb, and it changed how we light up our world. Before the light bulb, we used candles or oil lamps when it got dark. But thanks to Edison's invention, we can now turn on a light with a switch and banish the darkness.

Think about how cool the light bulb is. With a simple switch, our homes and cities light up with a warm, radiant glow. It's as if we have a tiny sun in a glass bulb that can make the dark go away and show us cool things even at night.

Edison's light bulb uses electricity to make light in a new and useful way. There's a thin part inside it that, when we give it electricity, gets really hot and gives off a bright light. This cool idea didn't just change our homes; it also changed how our workplaces, streets, and whole cities look. Now, we can do things and be creative even when it's dark outside.

The light bulb isn't just helpful; it's changed everything about how we live. It helped factories work all the time, making things faster. It made streets and public places safer by lighting them up. It also helped schools, libraries, and theaters stay open longer. So, turning on a light isn't just about seeing better; it's using a special power to make our world a brighter and cooler place, thanks to inventors like Thomas Edison.

The Internet and Computers: Transforming Our World

Computers are incredible tools that enhance our lives in countless ways, acting like modern-day wonders. They've become essential, serving as magical helpers in various tasks, from complex math to fostering creativity in storytelling, art, and games.

In education, computers have transformed learning, providing instant access to knowledge for tasks like solving math problems, creating stories, and exploring the universe through simulations. They've become companions on our journey of learning and self-discovery.

Beyond education, computers open the door to a world of entertainment, allowing us to play games, create digital art, and unleash our imaginations. Additionally, the internet, like a giant library that never closes, offers endless information on various subjects, transcending geographical barriers and connecting people globally. It enables real-time conversations and access to diverse perspectives, making us feel connected worldwide.

In essence, computers and the internet are more than tools; they're companions, windows to the world, and catalysts for progress. Created to improve our lives, they continue evolving, pushing the boundaries of what's possible and shaping our lives in ways we can only imagine.

Everyday Innovations: The Power of Small Inventions

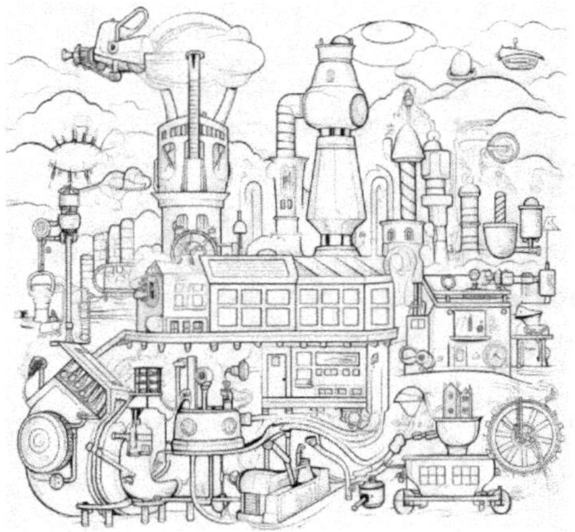

In our world of big and exciting things, we sometimes forget about the simple inventions that make our lives better every day. Things like the zipper, traffic lights, and popsicles might seem small, but they are important parts of our daily routines, bringing us joy and making things easier.

Take the humble zipper, for example. It's a tiny but super useful thing that helps us fasten our clothes and bags easily. No more struggling with buttons and laces – getting dressed becomes a breeze. Even small inventions like this can make a big difference in our lives.

Then there are traffic lights. They're silent helpers on the roads, ensuring cars and people move safely. They prevent accidents and keep things in order at busy intersections. It's amazing how something so simple can make our cities safer.

And who doesn't love popsicles? These frozen treats on a stick bring so much happiness, especially on hot summer days. They show us that inventions can be simple but really enjoyable, making our lives a little sweeter.

Inventors are like secret heroes. They turn their ideas into real things, making the world better. They solve problems we might not even know we have.

As you go through your day, remember that even small inventions can be super cool. And who knows, maybe one day, you'll come up with an amazing invention that changes how we live. Keep dreaming big, stay curious, and keep exploring the world of awesome inventions!

8 | Travel Adventures

Hello, young globetrotters! Get ready for an exciting chapter filled with travel adventures that will transport you to different countries and cultures around the world. We'll dive deeper into fascinating facts and explore the wonders of these amazing places. It's a whirlwind tour without leaving your chair, so buckle up for an enriching journey!

The Great Pyramids of Egypt: Pyramid Puzzles

Welcome to a magical journey to Egypt, where we're going to discover the incredible Great Pyramids! Imagine these pyramids as gigantic towers, but they are not made of glass and steel; they were built a very, very long time ago.

These pyramids are special because people think they were made as huge, magnificent tombs for very important people called pharaohs. Pharaohs were Kings of ancient Egypt, and they ruled the land a long, long time ago.

Now, picture this: you are an adventurer like Indiana Jones, and get to go inside these pyramids! Waiting inside is a giant puzzle for you to solve. There are secret rooms and tunnels that make you feel like an archaeologist, which is a fancy word for someone who discovers old things buried underground.

Colorful India: Festival of Colors

Holi is a day of jubilation and merrymaking that is observed by the entire town. It's a day when people come together to play with colorful powders, ranging from red, blue, green, and more. Colorful water balloons are also popular, and participants throw them at each other, creating a lively atmosphere that's full of laughter and joy. It's a giant paint war, but with a happy twist!

During Holi, the streets come alive with a myriad of vibrant colors as people cover their faces and clothes in bright hues. It's a sight to behold as the entire town transforms into a magnificent, living painting, with everyone taking part in the festivities!

Holi is more than just a celebration of color; it's about coming together with your loved ones, enjoying delectable treats, and dancing to lively tunes. Imagine being a part of the world's most spectacular color explosion and having an absolute blast!

If you ever visit India during Holi, get ready to join in the colorful fun and celebrate the joy of togetherness with people who love making the world a more colorful and happy place!

Japan's Mount Fuji: Majestic Mountain

Mount Fuji is not just any mountain; it's a super-tall volcano that stands tall and proud. It's the highest mountain in all of Japan! Sometimes, it's covered in a beautiful white blanket of snow, making it look like a giant ice cream cone. Yum!

Mount Fuji holds a special place in the hearts of the Japanese as a symbol of the nation's beauty and grace. Gazing upon this majestic mountain, one might feel as though they have been transported to a whimsical fairy tale land.

There are some adventurous souls that decide to climb Mount Fuji. The summit rewards climbers with breathtaking views that surpass even those seen from an airplane window. Reaching the top of Mount Fuji is like standing on top of the world!

So, when you visit Japan and see Mount Fuji, remember that it's not just a mountain; it's a symbol of beauty, and it's waiting for you to explore its majesty!

Brazilian Carnival: Samba Showtime

Let's picture a magnificent parade where people are adorned in the most stunning and breathtaking costumes you've ever seen. These outfits are so elaborate that they sparkle like a million stars in the sky, leaving a lasting impression on anyone who sees them. Each person looks like a real-life superhero, but instead of capes, they wear feathers, sequins, and sparkles that make them stand out from the crowd

And the music! Oh, the music is like magic. It fills the air with excitement and makes your toes tap and your hips sway. It's so catchy that you can't help but dance along! The whole city comes alive with the sound of drums, trumpets, and joyful singing.

The best part of Carnival? The samba dance! It's like a dance party all on its own - fast-paced and exhilarating. Watching the samba dancers spin, twirl, and move with such speed and precision creates a whirlwind of joy and rhythm that will make your heart race with delight.

Greece: Land of Ancient Myths

Once upon a time, the Greeks shared fascinating tales of gods and goddesses similar to superheroes possessing remarkable powers. Among them, Zeus reigned supreme, his wave of the hand producing thunder and lightning! Meanwhile, the super-strong Hercules performed incredible feats of heroism. These larger-than-life figures were the ultimate action stars in their own epic tales.

The Parthenon, one of the many stunning structures from ancient Greece, is a sight to behold and seems to be straight out of a fairy tale. The grand building was constructed using white marble and is akin to a massive puzzle made up of intricately fitting pieces. It's so breathtaking that it would seem like a palace fit for the gods themselves!

Traveling to Greece is like entering a storybook filled with epic tales and secrets of ancient times. You can explore the very same temples and buildings that the Greeks constructed thousands of years ago, and immerse yourself in their art, music, and remarkable inventions.

Pack your bags and get ready for a journey to Greece, where you'll uncover the mysteries of an ancient civilization and meet some of the coolest heroes and gods from the past! It's a magical place where history comes to life, and you're the explorer of a fantastic world of myths and legends!

The Great Wall of China: Wall of Wonders

Visualize a magnificent wall that stretches across mountains, hills, and valleys, like a magical road winding through the stunning landscapes of China. What's more, this isn't an ordinary wall. It's an ancient, centuries-old structure that has stood the test of time.

The Great Wall of China: A Symbol of Human Ingenuity and Cooperation In ancient times, the Chinese constructed a wall to protect their homeland from outside threats. This remarkable fortification represents the strength and resilience of humanity when working together towards a common goal. The wall, made of bricks and stones, stands as a testament to the intelligence and determination of the Chinese people.

Now, here's the coolest part: when you walk along the Great Wall, you're walking through history. You can feel the stories of all the people who built it and protected China with their hard work. It's almost like stepping into a time machine and going back in time to see how things were a long, long time ago.

Traveling to different places helps us learn about how people live, their traditions, and the amazing things they've created. Every place we visit has its own special stories and wonders to share. Even if you can't go on real adventures right now, we can still explore and learn about all the incredible places and people that make our world so exciting and diverse!

9 | Puzzles and Brain Teasers

Hello, young puzzle masters! In this topic, we're going to embark on a journey filled with brain-boggling fun, exciting quizzes, tricky riddles, and engaging puzzles that will both tickle your brain and test your knowledge. Are you ready to dive into the world of challenges, mystery-solving, and having a blast along the way? Let's get started!

Riddles, the Brain Ticklers

Riddles are like fun puzzles for your brain! They ask tricky questions that make you think hard, and when you figure them out, it feels like you've won a special prize for your brain.

Here's a riddle for you to solve: What has keys but can't open locks? Think about it for a moment. Give up? Well, the answer is… a piano! That's right, a piano has keys like a keyboard, but those keys can't open any locks. Isn't that clever?

1. I'm full of keys, but I can't open any locks. What am I?

2. I'm tall when I'm young, and short when I'm old. What am I?

3. What comes once in a minute, twice in a moment, but never in a thousand years?

4. I have keys but can't open locks. You can enter, but you can't go inside. What am I?

5. I'm black and white and loved by pandas. What am I?

6. I'm full of holes, but I can still hold water. What am I?

7. I'm always hungry, I must always be fed. The finger I touch, will soon turn red. What am I?

8. I'm a fruit with a yellow peel and white inside. I'm a favorite snack for monkeys. What am I?

9. I have keys but can't open locks. I'm found in your pocket, and I tell you the time. What am I?

10. I'm a type of animal with a long neck and spots. What am I?

Find the answers for these questions at the end of this chapter.

Crossword Puzzles, Word Magic

Hey there, word explorers! Let's dive into the enchanting world of crossword puzzles.

Picture a grid that looks like a big checkerboard with tiny squares. Some of these squares have numbers, and your job is to fill them with special words. But here's the tricky part: the words need to fit both across and down, like roads in a puzzle city.

Imagine you have a bunch of word clues, like secret messages waiting to be discovered. These clues tell you what words to find and where to put them in the grid. It's like a treasure hunt, but instead of hunting for gold, you're hunting for words!

Each word is like a puzzle piece, and as you fill in the grid, a magical picture will appear. You're not just finding words; you're building a word wonderland!

Crossword puzzles are not just games; they're vocabulary adventures. They help you learn new words and how to spell them. Plus, they're super satisfying because when you solve a clue, you can have a little victory dance in your brain!

You can do crossword puzzles by yourself or with friends and family. You can even find them in newspapers, books, or online.

ANIMALS

ACROSS

2. A cousin to apes
4. Flying mammal
5. A large animal that lives in deserts
7. Likes to chase mice
8. Large marsupial

DOWN

1. Man's best friend
3. Has a trunk
4. A furry animal with a big flat tail and large teeth
6. A large cat

Sudoku, Number Challenge

Hello, little number wizards! Let's dive into the world of Sudoku, the amazing number challenge that will make your brain feel like it's doing magic with numbers.

Imagine a big square divided into smaller squares, like a puzzle made of boxes. Your job is to fill in these boxes with numbers. But here's the catch: you need to use the numbers 1 through 9, and you can't use any of them more than once in each row, column, or little square. It's like a magical number rule!

Sudoku puzzles come in different sizes and difficulties, from easy-peasy to super challenging. You can start with the easier ones and become a real number wizard as you tackle the trickier ones!

Sudoku is not just a game; it's a number puzzle that exercises your brain. It helps you become better at math and problem-solving, and it's so satisfying when you complete a puzzle.

You can find Sudoku puzzles in puzzle books, newspapers, or online. You can even create your own mini Sudoku puzzles on a piece of paper! You're being a mathematician on a quest for numerical excellence.

So, the next time you see a Sudoku puzzle, give it a try! You can try and become a number wizard. Have a blast with Sudoku!

SUDOKU PUZZLE

Fill in the puzzle so that every row across, every column down and
every 9 by 9 box contains the numbers 1 to 9.

9	6					2		3
3					8		5	6
5	1			6		8	4	
2			7	4	1	6	8	
7	5	6						1
4		1			2			9
	9	5				3	7	
6			4	3	5	1		
	4	3	1			5	6	

Brain Teasers, Mind Games

Brain teasers are like mini-games for your brilliant brain. They encourage creative thinking and clever problem-solving.

Here's one to spark your imagination: You see a boat filled with people. It hasn't sunk, but when you look again, you don't see a single person on the boat. Why is that?

Answer: They're all married

Puzzles and brain teasers are like a workout for your brain. They're incredibly fun, and they offer fantastic benefits, helping you learn new things, develop critical thinking skills, and enjoy yourself all at the same time. So, prepare to challenge yourself, solve mysteries, and become a true puzzle-solving pro!

ANSWERS TO PAGE 73

1. A piano
2. A candle
3. The letter "M"
4. A keyboard
5. A Bamboo
6. A Sponge
7. Fire
8. A Banana
9. A Watch
10. A giraffe

ANSWERS TO PAGE 76

ANSWERS TO PAGE 78

9	6	8	5	7	4	2	1	3
3	7	4	2	1	8	9	5	6
5	1	2	3	6	9	8	4	7
2	3	9	7	4	1	6	8	5
7	5	6	9	8	3	4	2	1
4	8	1	6	5	2	7	3	9
1	9	5	8	2	6	3	7	4
6	2	7	4	3	5	1	9	8
8	4	3	1	9	7	5	6	2

10 | Amazing Sports and Games

Hey there, sports and games enthusiasts! In this topic, we're going to explore the exciting world of sports, games, and the incredible athletes who play them. Get ready for a fun-filled journey of facts from around the globe!

Sports, the Ultimate Fun

Hey there, future sports champs! Let's dive into the exciting world of sports, where fun and adventure go hand in hand

In a world full of games where people come together to run, jump, kick, and play. These games are called sports, some are quite similar and some are quite different but there are sports for everyone to enjoy.

Teamwork

Teamwork is a central component of many sports. Athletes work together as a tightknit unit, not unlike a supportive family, to achieve a common goal of winning the game.

Different Sports

There are so many sports to choose from! You can play soccer, where you kick a ball into a goal. You can shoot hoops in basketball, or you can race to the finish line in track and field. You have a whole buffet of fun games to pick from!

Staying Healthy

Playing sports not only provides fun and social connections but also enhances overall health and fitness by building strength, endurance, flexibility, and coordination. It boosts the immune system, reduces the risk of diseases, and improves mental health while reducing stress levels.

Fun for Everyone

Regardless of age or background, sports offer an excellent way to stay active and engaged. You have access to an enormous playground where everyone can participate and enjoy themselves.

Big Events

Every four years, people get together from all over the world to compete in different sports at the Olympics, where athletes show off their amazing skills.

Sports are not just about winning; they're about playing, making friends, and enjoying the thrill of the game. It's one big adventure where you get to be a hero on the field or the court.

The next time you see a soccer ball, a basketball, or a race track, remember that it's an invitation to join in the ultimate fun – sports! Get ready to run, jump, and score some goals, because sports are where the magic of teamwork and having a blast come alive!

The Olympics, a Worldwide Party

The Olympics are a gigantic sports party where people from all around the world come together to play their favorite sports. Think of it as a mega-sports celebration!

Global Gathering

Athletes from hundreds of countries travel to one place to show off their skills. It's like having a huge sports reunion with friends from all over the globe.

Lots of Sports

There are many sports at the Olympics. You've got swimming, gymnastics, running, and even jumping really far! There's a plethora of sports to watch and cheer for.

Team Spirit

Each athlete represents their own country, but they also make new friends from different places. Athletes from different countries come together as everyone is friendly and supportive.

Medals and Awards

Athletes try their very best to win medals. Gold, silver, and bronze medals are given to those finishing in first, second and third.

Opening Ceremony

The Olympics start with a grand show called the Opening Ceremony. It kickoffs the Olympics with music, dancing, and lots of excitement.

Sportsmanship

The Olympics are not just about winning; they're also about playing fair, being kind, and showing respect to others. It's helps people learn good sportsmanship.

So, when you see the Olympic rings or hear about the games, get ready for weeks of sports you can watch. You'll get to see people from all over the world come together to cheer, laugh, and enjoy the amazing world of sports. Get ready to be part of this awesome sports party!

Soccer, the Global Game

Soccer is a sport that people all over the world go crazy for. It's the number one game on our planet! People from nearly every country play and watch soccer. Some people call it football and some people call it soccer depending on where they are from.

Global Love

Soccer is loved by so many people in almost every corner of the world. It brings everyone together in excitement and joy.

World Cup

Have you heard of the FIFA World Cup? It's the biggest soccer party on the planet! Teams from different countries come to play in this amazing tournament. People from all over the globe tune in to watch.

Simple and Fun

You don't need fancy equipment to play soccer. All you need is a ball and some friends. Anyone can join in and have a blast.

Teamwork

Soccer is not just about kicking the ball into the goal. It's also about working together as a team. Each team is made. of eleven friends who support each other on and off the field.

Passion and Pride

When people talk about their favorite soccer teams, they're talking about family. There's so much passion and pride in supporting your team, and fans wear their team's colors with pride.

The next time you see a soccer ball or a soccer match on TV remember it's all about having fun, being active, and cheering for your team. Join in with the soccer excitement!

Cool Games from Around the World

Hey there, young adventurers! Let's embark on a journey to discover cool games from around the world. Each country has its unique games that are loads of fun.

Sumo Wrestling in Japan

Witness as enormous and powerful wrestlers, donned in special belts, battle it out to push each other out of a sand-filled ring. This super-sized wrestling match is like nothing else, a spectacle that can only be described as having human giant teddy bears collide!

Kabaddi in India

Here's a fun one! Players take turns running into the other team's territory, tagging as many opponents as they can, and then racing back to their side while holding their breath. It's a thrilling game of tag mixed with holding your breath underwater!

Holi Festival in India

Don't forget about the Festival of Colors in India that we discussed earlier! In addition to Holi, there are also water balloon fights in which people fill balloons with colorful water and toss them at their friends. It's a playful and vibrant water battle that everyone can enjoy.

Marbles in the Philippines

Have you heard of "holen" or marbles in the Philippines? Players aim to eliminate their opponent's marbles by using their own to knock them out of a circle. It's a game that requires strategy and precision, making it a thrilling competition of skill.

Jump Rope in the USA

Jump rope games are popular in many places, including the United States. Kids swing a rope, and you have to jump over it without tripping. It's a rhythmic dance with a rope!

Tug of War

Tug of war is a worldwide classic game where two teams pull on opposite ends of a rope, with the strongest team emerging victorious. It's essentially a massive game of "who's the strongest?"

Games provide insight into diverse cultures, promoting physical activity, mental stimulation, teamwork, creativity, and strategic thinking. They bridge cultural gaps, break language barriers, and connect people worldwide. Some games reflect religious or social beliefs, like Mahjong, while others, like soccer, have a rich history and global appeal. Advancements in technology and transportation have led to new games, including online and virtual reality games, offering immersive experiences that challenge players in unprecedented ways.

Amazing Athletes

Think of athletes as people who are great at playing sports. They train hard, which means they practice a lot to become the best at what they do. The saying goes "practice makes perfect" and they certainly practie a lot.

Now, let's meet some superstar athletes:

Usain Bolt

He's known as the fastest man on Earth! Imagine running so fast that you leave everyone else behind like a flash of lightning. Usain Bolt can do that, and he's super inspiring!

Simone Biles

She's a gymnastics superstar. Imagine doing flips, twists, and turns in the air, and landing gracefully like a feather. Simone Biles is incredibly talented, and her gymnastics routines are like magic!

LeBron James

He's a basketball legend. Picture dribbling the basketball, making amazing shots, and helping your team win. LeBron James does that and more. He's a basketball wizard!

Serena Williams

She's a tennis champion. Tennis is a game of skill, where you need to hit the ball just right. Serena Williams is a master at it, and her tennis moves are poetry in motion!

Michael Phelps

He's a fish in the water! Imagine swimming so fast that you win twenty three gold medals. Michael Phelps is an incredible swimmer, and he's won more medals than anyone else in history with twenty eight!

These athletes are like role models because they show us that with hard work, dedication, and a lot of passion, we can achieve amazing things too. They inspire us to aim high and dream big!

Paralympics: A Triumph of Human Potential and Unity

The Paralympics, also known as the "parallel games" to the Olympics, are an amazing celebration of diversity, ability, and strength. In these special events, athletes with disabilities compete at the highest level, showing us that they can achieve incredible things and proving that the human spirit is unbeatable.

In the Paralympics, the playing field is leveled not by reducing the athletes' abilities, but by highlighting their exceptional talents and strong determination. Each athlete, no matter their challenges, teaches us that striving for excellence has no limits. They show us that obstacles can be overcome, and dreams can come true.

The Paralympics go beyond just showing athletic skills; they celebrate the triumph of the human spirit over challenges. These athletes inspire us with their resilience, teaching us that with passion, dedication, and believing in ourselves, we can overcome anything life throws our way.

In sports and games, we discover a universal language that brings people together, no matter their background or abilities. Whether it's a fun soccer game in the park or a fantastic Paralympic event on TV, sports have a special way of capturing our hearts and motivating us to aim for greatness.

Watching these incredible athletes on the world stage reminds us that sports are not just about winning or losing; they're about the journey, dedication, and the shared human experience. The Paralympics show us how sports can unite athletes with different abilities, letting them showcase their talents, celebrate their achievements, and inspire all of us to reach for the stars.

11 | Mythical Creatures

Welcome to the fascinating world of mythical creatures! In this chapter, we'll journey into the realm of legends and myths from various cultures to discover some of the most extraordinary beings ever imagined. These creatures are part of ancient stories that have been passed down through generations, filling our world with wonder and mystery.

Dragons: Fire-Breathing Serpents

Dragons are fascinating, make-believe creatures that people have talked about for a really long time. They resemble giant, flying snakes that can breathe out fire, just like a flamethrower!

People from different parts of the world have shared stories about dragons. In China, some think dragons are wise and bring good luck, similar to a good-luck charm. They see dragons as friendly and nice creatures.

But in other stories, especially in the Western part of the world, dragons aren't so friendly. They often play the role of the bad guys in fairy tales and have battles with brave knights and heroes.

Dragons are these magical beings that can be good or bad, depending on the story. One thing is for sure: they're always super big and can breathe fire!

Unicorns: The Enchanted Ones

Unicorns are enchanting creatures, resembling magical horses but with something extra special – a single, twisty horn on their foreheads. A beautiful horse with a shiny, spiral horn right in the middle of its head!

People have talked about unicorns for a really long time, thinking of them as pure and graceful creatures. It's as if they're always on their best behavior, similar to the nicest and most polite horse you can think of.

Unicorns are these magical, one-horned horses all about being pure and graceful. They bring a touch of wonder to the world with their magical horn!

A long time ago, some folks believed that unicorn horns had super cool powers. They thought unicorn horns could heal people when they were sick and even make dirty water all clean and fresh! How handy that would be!

Griffins: Majestic Half-Bird, Half-Beast

Griffins are mythical creatures that combine features of lions and eagles. A lion with a head like an eagle and big, strong wings!

Griffins are extraordinary beings in the animal kingdom, recognized for their strength, bravery, and unwavering loyalty. They're like steadfast companions, always having your back.

In ancient times, people believed griffins served as guardians for special treasures, acting as secret protectors. Having an image of a griffin was thought to keep valuable items safe.

What's impressive about griffins is how they bring together the best qualities of lions and eagles. Lions are strong and fierce, eagles are swift and can fly high – griffins combine both, symbolizing bravery and power.

Having a griffin as a friend would make you feel incredibly safe and strong!

Phoenixes: Rebirth from the Ashes

Phoenixes are mythical birds with a remarkable power – they can return to life after turning into ashes, getting a fresh start!

In stories, when a phoenix becomes really old, it does something extraordinary. It bursts into flames and becomes ashes, similar to burning a piece of paper. The incredible part is that from those ashes, a brand new baby phoenix emerges, young and full of life!

This uniqueness makes phoenixes special by teaching us that regardless of age or weariness, there's always a chance to start anew and be fresh.

People in different places adore the idea of phoenixes because they remind us that we can continuously renew ourselves and keep going, just like the phoenix. They serve as a symbol of never giving up and always having a chance to start over.

Mermaids: Mystical Ocean Dwellers

Mermaids are fantastical sea creatures, combining human and fish parts with a person on top and a fishy tail on the bottom!

Deeply connected to the sea, they're renowned for enchanting songs that captivate sailors, sometimes leading them into trouble. Their voice is thought to be magic!

Part of stories and legends for a very long time, sailors exploring the vast ocean often dream of encountering these captivating beings. Storytellers are drawn to tales about them because of their mysterious and magical nature.

These incredible creatures, part-human and part-fish, reside in the sea, singing lovely songs and inspiring countless stories. They are the ocean's magical stars!

Minotaurs: Half-Man, Half-Bull

Minotaurs are mythical creatures with a unique appearance – a person's body and a head resembling a big, strong bull with horns.

One of the most famous minotaurs lived in a labyrinth on the island of Crete in ancient Greece. This minotaur, a mix of human and bull, was known to be incredibly strong and a bit scary.

Legend has it that the minotaur was born due to a curse, a magical spell gone wrong. A hero named Theseus, who was super brave, entered the labyrinth and defeated the minotaur. It's an exciting adventure story!

Minotaurs symbolize the wild and sometimes scary parts of nature, reminding us to be careful and not let untamed things get out of control. Despite their strange appearance, minotaurs have fascinating stories that offer important lessons to be cautious, safe and making the right choices.

Kitsune: Clever Fox Spirits

Kitsune are magical foxes from captivating stories in Japan. They're not ordinary foxes – incredibly smart and capable of magic tricks!

One fascinating aspect of kitsune is their ability to change shape. Picture a fox turning into a human, a magical disguise! They use this power for fun and to play tricks on people, embodying mischievous little pranksters.

But that's not their only role. Kitsune also assist in caring for special places and delivering messages for an important god called Inari in the Shinto religion. They can be seen as guardian figures too!

Kitsune are a blend of playful and mysterious, adding a touch of magic to Japanese stories, enhancing their excitement and enchantment.

Krakens: Giant Sea Monsters

Krakens are enormous and frightening sea creatures living deep in the ocean. Storytellers describe them with long, twisty arms capable of grabbing and pulling ships underwater. That would be incredibly spooky if it were real!

People from faraway places, like Scandinavia and Norseland, used to share stories about krakens. Sailors hearing these tales got really scared, thinking a kraken might appear while they were sailing on the ocean.

Krakens are the kings of sea monsters, existing in stories for a very long time. Picture being on a ship, wondering if a giant kraken might show up! It's like a big, exciting adventure, even though krakens are just in stories.

Even though krakens aren't real, they showcase how creative our minds can be. People love inventing stories about these incredible creatures, giving us exciting tales and legends. So, explore your imagination, and maybe you'll discover more mythical creatures in the world of stories!

CONCLUSION

And there you have it, young explorers and knowledge seekers! We've embarked on a thrilling journey through these pages. From the wonders of nature to the mysteries of space, from incredible inventions to mythical creatures, this book has been your trusty guide to a world filled with knowledge, adventure, and wonder.

As you close these pages, remember that the world is a treasure trove of fascinating facts, and your curiosity is the key to unlocking its secrets. Whether you're discovering the mysteries of space or unraveling the tales of mythical creatures, never stop exploring, asking questions, and seeking knowledge.

Every fact you've learned, every story you've read, and every question you've asked has brought you one step closer to becoming a lifelong learner, an intrepid explorer, and a true adventurer in the world of knowledge. So, keep your eyes wide open, your mind ever curious, and your heart forever eager to learn.

The world is your playground, and the pursuit of knowledge is your greatest adventure. As you grow and explore, may the wonders of the world continue to amaze you, and may your thirst for knowledge always lead you on exciting journeys.

Thank you for joining us on this incredible ride through this book. Now, go out into the world and let your curiosity shine as you uncover even more fascinating facts and embark on countless adventures of your own.

Happy exploring, young adventurers, and remember: The world is full of wonders waiting for you to discover!